For The Time Being

Stephen Bailey

Published by
Ararua Books, Ōtaki, Aotearoa

ISBN 978-0-473-67118-1

For Judy
on our
30th wedding anniversary

17 April 2023

*In Māori cosmology creation is detailed as a whakapapa, which
outlines the numerous generations of Te Kore (the void), Te Pō
(the night) and Te Ao (the day). The text of the chant runs as an
undercurrent through this book briefly appearing and developing
in the interludes between the sections.*

Prefatory Note
Parallels as a poetics

In dialogue, a key feature of the form: to speak within
as twinned; or, with another as a twin; Plato's mode of
philosophical question that defined Western reason
through artful interrogative pattern. A call and
response, response and call, echoes of question and
answer in each poem, the plural of voices in mutual
exchange: *dia* through *logos* speech, reason; dialogos.

    blind
    with words

            a poet sounds out

    whispered
    in darkness

            the songs
            being silenced

    singed
    with light

            breath by breath

The poetic form presented within is newly minted, yet
draws on a redoubtable haiku tradition. Speaking
doubly—poet to shadow, man to *ecos* and world; human
to the sacred, and what is most human to the sacred; as
wood to pine; sky to life. In dialogue too with suffering
and death.

same old valley

it's all
about me

a transfiguring
moon

thy kingdom
that is not

silences me

of this world

I feel the years of contemplation involved producing
this creative work. Poems unsuitable as tweets, each
meant to be left with you: alone for a while. Just let it
sink in without scrolling.

A parallel-form poetics presents dual mirrors of the
soul, a seeing through seeing through one voice in
counterpoint with another that hits deeply enough: the
root of selves. It's often a jarring and sudden style, the
in-between molecular layer of silver at the fulcrum of
two polarities that we are, both within in revealed layers
at our core, and whatever is that voice returning--two
sorts of soul or persona, in the same moment speaking
through each other—let us question at every point, in
every line the question of arrival.

You, reader, may never finish this book, unless like an animal extinction, the poetic force leaves you, and you turn away from one poet's truth, a truth that comes not between you and him, but between us all. May you find though these novel investigations ways to speak doubly, in dialogue, you and that other you—the following pages of illumination to guide you.

> make a name
> for yourself

> > *with tongue-tripping*
> > *skips*

> imprint
> your presence
> into

> > *from lips*
> > *to petrichor*

> our hearts
> of stone

> > *rain's*
> > *pitter-patter*

Richard Gilbert, PhD
Co-Editor of *Heliosparrow Poetry Journal*
Author of *The Disjunctive Dragonfly, Poems of Consciousness & Poetry as Consciousness*

Ko Te Kore (the void, energy, nothingness, potential)
Te Kore-te-whiwhia (the void in which nothing is possessed)
Te Kore-te-rawea (the void in which nothing is felt)
Te Kore-i-ai (the void with nothing in union)
Te Kore-te-wiwia (the space without boundaries)
Na Te Kore Te Po (from the void the night)

being
in a

       all these words

present continuous
tense

       written for
       the time being

unfolding
rapture

       a creature
       of the now

in deep
water

human nature

the cold light
of day

surviving
the veneer

obscures
the cosmos

of identity

winter moon

        all the earth

the light-fingered
touch

        lost within
        the to
        and fro

of being
known

        of identity

winter scene

        all about

enter it

        my shadow
        deeper

through being
seen

        in withouts

not just
an oak

        here
        and now

but the
afterimage

        where a word
        separates

its name
paints

        then
        from now

sublime vacancy

        post-literate
        verse

I string time out
into metaphors

        all the white
        spaces

of distance

        fit together

distant past

              gone to seed

almost
remembered

              grasses
              on the graves

cicadas

              marked by
              my blood

family tree

my genome
traced

all the couplings

through red-fingered
ridges and whorls

that came
and went

in distant
cave walls

my forebears

the sun casts

long harvested
silence

its impression
of me

for its music

to the ground

infinite
immensity

> *a want*
> *of words*

dare I domesticate
the sublime

> *sublimating*
> *domestic*

in such
short measure

> *drudgery*

a chance
glance

for
heaven's sake

into
the origin

a tuatara's
lunge

of being

at self-awareness

overnight

gnostic night

the universe
rumbles out

interlocking
coffee stains

its origins

spill the beans

dust motes

black holes

our origins
red-shifted

my eyes
sieving light

through
the stars

from
the milky way

milk-heavy
cows

               a future
               passing

hauling
back home

               howls across

the
end of days

               the paddock

a butterfly

                    at the words

stilled

                    of consecration

on the altar

                    a gong sounds

childhood

               rock pool eyes

the tug

               my fingers
               explore

of a sea
anemone

               the tidal life

wood ear
fungus

              underfoot

the rainforest's

              the Isaiah
              Scroll's

prophetic
words

              dead sea
              of leaves

a dull chill

         is this
         not it

just the
dying away

         the clarity
         I keep losing

of lightning

         since I awoke?

winter sky

        two widows

in the market
for

        haggle over
        the price

bright colours

        of living
        alone

on my knees

between shifts

I gaze into
the depths

at the freezing
works

of stagnant words

I am
Raskolnikov

my parents
too

        howling storms

reduced to
the anonymity

        unearthing
        the phenomenon

of
just bones

        of man

babes suckle
on the silence

excruciating

of that which
permeates

time teeters
on the edge

everything

of tomorrow's
now

wiping out

   a blank slate

the last
traces

   I redraw

of this
breath

   a butterfly's
   flight

whisper it

        winter hush

when silence
is an echo

        long shadows
        offer up

of itself

        mute evidence

flitter-winged

in a blink

a butterfly
beyond

*the beginning
of time*

our here
& now

pinpointed

a butterfly

self-pity
swallows

navigating
a yester-dream

yet another
illusion

on borrowed
time

of being
apparent

words
which embody

a universe

our
very selves

edging to
the precipice

in screams
of newness

where words
wave back

what is this
breath?

           a fantail

a breach between

           teases out
           the mortality

then and now?

           moulded
           into me

a spring
storm

        childhood
        home

the sounds
of belonging

        the distance
        separating

back as new

        awake
        & asleep

boyhood dream

                Palmer's
                bright cloud

the future
creaks through

                that which
                I was

a rusted gate

                when still
                I wasn't

the sweetest
apple

my baby blue
eyes

doesn't fall
far from

bestow ancestral
blessings

the family tree

on all
they behold

a new dawn

        out of
        empty caves

hunter-gatherers

        a semblance
        of similarity

in long queues

        reassembling

detonated
by dawn

> *traveling*
> *godzone*

my dream

> *my urge*
> *to (t)read*

of self

> *between*
> *the lines*

overcast night

        grey matter

clouds darken
another half

        long lost
        memories

of the moon

        slip through
        my dreams

seen
darkly

a poem
reflects

an ugly
duckling

returning
wild swans

faintly
white

at Coole

vine-tangled
style

                    signposts

when did
anything

                    urge me
                    to tread

become mine?

                    between
                    the lines

bitter wind

        breaking light

calumny
hisses at me

        how I never
        longed to see

with
a human voice

        the face
        of evil

fog-addled brain—

        morning maze—

watching where
I walk

        a sense
        of belonging

I see clearly

        around the corner

wonder-wending

the all

rainforest trails

bottoms into

the child in me
I word

a wellspring

levelling up

noun or verb

I am who

the human
being

I have
always been

human
still

binary stars

        mayfly dance

my mind
interfaces with

        what once was

a world
of words

        will ever be

new moon

        all the other
        places

under the
weather vane

        I cannot
        also be

a wormhole

        in the present
        moment

sun and moon

        flaming bush

far from
the juniper shade

        I am
        being

a gentle breeze

        who I am

I am

        between
        our eyes

what you
are not

        the silence
        that passes

mirror
imaged

        for breath

between
breaths

        the oceanic
        swells

an underground
stream

        at the centre
        of the dream

of consciousness

        of being
        me

self-announcing

      into darkness

the morepork's

      the onomatopoeia

two-tone call

      of identity

the moonlight

        the holy grail

it is
the water

        at the
        very heart

in the bucket

        of becoming

soft
in the wind

stilled here

a tree-fern
tossing fronds

a vision
of self

of belonging

at shadow
play

westerly wind

        tuning fork

the resonance
of my breath

        one prong
        shorter

in
cupped hands

        than
        the other

parallel streams

      shifting weight

a boulder
takes on

      I stand for now

three dimensions

      on my own
      two feet

on a
white stone

immersed

your name

in the life of

before
baptism

the triune God

captivated

        in an instant

infinity
caught up

        I know myself

in marble

        without
        a name

an AI struts

all that's left

the theatre
of the absurd

just six characters

in search of
an author

for a passport
to the sublime

it's down

        poplars

in black
& white

        barcode

natural
codification

        the sun

dragonfly

a distant
mountain

my mind's
wide eyes

extrapolated

unseen

from
its reflection

birds of prey

        the bathos

compartmentalize

        peak moments
        enslaved

a dawn chorus

        in prattle

late night tryst

sound caught up

hear insects
lament

in the flow

the parting
still to come

*of continual
arrival*

night nature

        with sunset

the familiar
gnashes

        a dandelion
        goes into

its teeth

        stealth mode

hypostatic union

       just a rose leap

the otherness
within

       into
       the still point

a butterfly's
shadow

       of its scent

holy week

        a child singing

soul searching

        ring-a-ring
        o' roses

otherness

        all alone

trailing along

       rooted
       in their blood

the convoluted path

       my shadow
       stretches out

of a morning glory

       over
       my ancestor's graves

autumn morn

where presence

feijoa halves
sink

and absence
overlap

into
my porridge

a cloud's
shadow

groundswell

        a cicada's

the grassroots
hold it

        emerging voice

all together

        grows resonant

mirroring

        a blow
        by blow

it's self

        analysis

a leaf
in freefall

        of the west wind

as I sleep

          unmasked
          for now

the interminable
lengthening

          our
          existential

of my
toe nails

          solitude

fallen leaves

       the knowledge

every Eve
& Adam of us

       of knowing
       nothing

washed up

       nakedly

way back
then

> *drowned*
> *once more*

an infantile
obsession

> *in cascades*
> *of chatter*

with crickets

> *your naked*
> *innocence*

sultry field

        the play's
        the thing

paspalum
sticks

        to catch
        the conscience

on
my calves

        not only
        of kings

shift 9

(my adult life

followed by
a theory

an open
parenthesis

of everything

on fatherhood

piecing
together

        haiku path

the edges
of the universe

        from
        juxtaposition

man
& wife

        to conjunction

late frost

       a black hole

so many
now younger

       with nothing

than me

       to crow about

lifeless leaves

being now

how implacably
my skin

the am
which will have been

has grown old

becoming

worn
right down

          in my spirit

my dreams
pebble down

          I find
          the nowhere

a primal shore

          to hide

moon-sphere

lead us not

filling
the still-point

into verbal
booby-traps

of a blind spot

of the
inauthentic

hollowed
of words

> *here we are*
> *then*

these shapes
without form

> *the whimper*
> *at the end*

shades
without colour

> *of the*
> *baby boom*

latterday plague

> *while the fever*
> *burns*

the profits of doom
undone

> *across the brows*
> *of his people*

upon
the bat's back

> *Nero fiddles*
> *the books*

Ko Te Kore (the void, energy, nothingness, potential)
Te Kore-te-whiwhia (the void in which nothing is possessed)
Te Kore-te-rawea (the void in which nothing is felt)
Te Kore-i-ai (the void with nothing in union)
Te Kore-te-wiwia (the space without boundaries)
Na Te Kore Te Po (from the void the night)
Te Po-nui (the great night)
Te Po-roa (the long night)
Te Po-uriuri (the deep night)
Te Po-kerekere (the intense night)
Te Po-tiwhatiwha (the dark night)

nothing but
this crystal liturgy

it is said

clarinet, violin,
cello & piano

there shall be
no more time

in a tangle
of rainbows

beyond the abyss
of birds

forest fugue

      sunken theme

a woodwind rises
to the theme

      a little girl
      barely bobbing

at the
conductor's baton

      under
      the surface

startling light

                traces of

a flicker
flutters

                the physiognomy

in the void

                of darkness

an in-gasp

      the why

teeters
on the brink

      beyond all

of silence

      becauses

either-or

a cloud

a river
of stars

downsizes

overnight

its shadow

bobbing
through dreams

        one haiku

a refined
savagery

        will not be
        enough

that seems to be
words

        summer rain

autumn gloom

limestone cave

a shadow
passes

a slow drip
joining the high

for a god

to the low

dew-less web

        at bird-hush

a landslide
victory

        a rainbow rages
        against the dying

for the
waking day

        of the light

under
the blossoms

           without ploughing
           I eat

Issa tosses
and turns

           the little
           red hen's bread

"I'm so afraid!"

           it's a wonder

candle flicker

        dusk-drawn
        hues

a moth's
momentum

        a roosting dove
        enfolds

shifting shadows

        the name
        of God

I awaken

   against
   the adulteration

to feel
emptiness

   of childlike wonder

yanked
out of me

   my lipids
   are steeled

a twist
of light

          conjugating verbs
          to be

the beginnings
of being

          sometimes
          I forget

a pine
at dawn

          that i'm
          awake

before dawn

        stillborn day

enlightenment
awakens

        a cockroach
        scuttles

to a drone
attack

        from
        the glare

less lost
than a lamb

        event horizon

my beatific vision

        I hover
        on the brink

in spring snow

        of an absence

wind-blown
shadows

the rusty chain

split under
the rising sun

clangs into
the sound

a fork-tongued
love

of a hollow
gong

utterly spent

        his little
        death

my ardour
wilts

        Hine-nui-te-pō
        exults

within her

        within me

Hemi
sphere

        Meri
        sphere

a fallen
hatching

        the soup kitchen

nests
in my palm

        almost smells
        like home

never lost

encrypted roadmap

a sparrow
flitting

is this
the colour

in the cat's
eyes

of blue?

deep reflection

       I strike a pose

a praying mantis

       with the poise

poised to strike

       of a shadow

at worship

awestruck

warships
passing

by the either-ors
of water

in
a dark night

from a rowboat

dewdrops

spring

straining

becomes

their surface
tension

*present
tense*

spring light

        tinting
        the bed

clearer
than ever

        with a lightness
        of touch

from above

        the river's
        flow

full of
moon

a shift

an absence
of such

of attentive
presence

not
so-noticed

to nothing

in two minds

      all the deaths

Mount Taranaki
by day

      I journey towards

by night

      auld lang syne

river fog

        fjord cataract

before
& after

        the logic
        of the moist eye

swamp hens

        blurring
        the edges

to be

            not to be

traces
of swan-glide

            a tomorrow

slashed
in water

            that
            never ends

staccato-blooded

martyr-made

cry st church
mosques

half a century

writing
my nation's story

at prayer

late cold snap

> *more*
> *than an echo*

each breath
becoming

> *the morepork*
> *foreshadowing*

what it's not

> *my near*
> *absence*

a failing light

                    a silhouette

dusts the real

                    settles down

with moths
of dream

                    on a wet
                    black bough

less & less

                a pause

echoes the call

                deeper into

of the wild

                between

morning fog

                    a tear

once words
for desolation

                    drops into
                    the stillness

have run
their course

                    of its absence

after dark

        Adam
        chthonic

the drip
drip drip

        explicates
        his origins

of dewfall

        with periods
        of silence

an owl
and I

here
and now

transfixed
on stars

the silence
I neglected

shining
in the past

to mention

moonlit quest

wind-watching

a fantail
in the shadows

*winter's
expiration*

my every move

*destroys
death*

waning moon

        is this
        what aging is?

its presence
wavering

        to be heartily sick
        of living

on the lapping
waves

        and yet
        and yet

the gap begins

                filling in
                the white space

with darkness
upon the face

                between fragment
                and phrase

of the deep

                a black hole

mid-morning
moon

                    my vision

a cloud
like

                    glances
                    the edge

no other

                    of remembering

soughing field

        vine-ripened

are these
but the sighs

        the tomato
        in her belly

of spent youth

        carried full-term

rose-fingered
dawn

> *blood-soaked*
> *earth*

the rupture
between then

> *which*
> *waving poppies*

& now

> *failed to let*
> *go of*

a warm front

        wind change

traces
its shadow

        I pass on

into
my will

        my reflection

my reflection

a mirror

then another
of me

*held up
to nature*

puddle
by puddle

*rippling from ear
to ear*

with an ear

                    mouthing sounds

to the silence

                    to a metronome

the owl's prey

                    my inner self

dark sky
viewing

        the world
        our oyster

I gulp at
the singularity

        and this awful
        loneliness

when space was
not yet

        words
        barely conceal

river estuary

        one hour's light

you will know
right away

        left

when you
get there

        the sun sinks there
        first

breath
of wind

        cave shadows

all lets go
bit by bit

        each comes
        to bear

everything

        a new name

late-life spring

        as near as
        a shadow

my other self

        the outgoing tide

neighbours
Bashō

        of the future

vernal equinox

        spring-stepped

cerebral
hemispheres

        a sexagenarian

launch
a new whole

        crosses
        the line

spring interlude

      within the space

I loose arrows

      between two
      hemispheres

along Zeno's
paradox

      I *divine*
      the whole

cicada shell

       god-forsaken

I am
nowhere

       the dessicated husk

to be seen

       on a tree

new year

timefall

a glance
tossed backwards

knowing
& unknowing

with 2020 vision

sharing
the same root

every Hansel
and Gretel

        stockpiling
        breadcrumbs

eating ourselves

        in labyrinthine

out of house
and home

        money trails

proclaiming

in the red corner

true justice
to the peoples

the prince of lies
exultant

a ruthless
silence

as a cancer

golden-topped
'shrooms

        left to rot

devout atheists
consume

        the last remnants

garden gods

        of that
        which fell

all over

      at odds with

the issue
of being

      the sophistry
      of in-turned eyes

a fog
of words

      sublime cosmos

nothing but

       the silence

a dragonfly

       when it was
       still

oviposting

       an after-thought

deep night
vigil

        sounds
        within

a flightless
bird

        the sounds
        without

rises
within

        something slips
        in-between

winter wind

          before the
          beginning

a rainbow
wilts

          and after
          the end

its being
present

          a rumble
          of becoming

night-writing

by a stretch

self-mutilation

of the
imagination

word
by word

daylight saving

have you come

            bequeath
            your wings

to complete
our haiku

            to my
            borrowed words

red dragonfly?

            red pepper

without
an end

        out on a limb

ants trailing
from the hole

        facing the infinite

without
a sound

        Ozaki Hōsai

a cunning
tongue

        behind blue eyes

explores
the tonality

        a butterfly's
        shadow

of my silence

        fanning me

in a pond

        having come
        thus far

I happen across

        these verses

my long-time
no-see look

        I am
        now writing

looking
like it

        the sun
        lingers

a pine cone
has become

        over a mountain's

fire

        loneliness

by moonlight

the divining rod

a poet
harvests

directing
his path

his field
of dreams

sounds like
silence

falling leaves

       a bell tolls

with a truth
too deep

       both near
       and far

for tears

       I am not
       an island

autumn dusk

         aging eyes

starlings bleed
tree-wards

         my mindscape
         dotted with

from the edge

         vanishing points

beyond being

        immune

useful members
of society

        from herd mentality

autumn leaves

        my secret room

a leaf escapes

        avenging angel

the endless
looping

        a nasal swab

of seasons

        sounds
        the all clear

wind-leaf breeze

        the chaos

her fingers
aflutter

        of unbecoming

speechless

        all fixed

leaden sky

                a spider

an illumined
lunacy

                unravels
                the physics

yields
the gold

                of fog

cosmic dust

        God's presence

a free-floating
comma

        tasted only

eats
roots & leaves

        at the speed
        of light

visions bob

       hypnic jerk

in omniscient
streams

       did I once
       fall asleep

below
the surface

       in a tree?

the mark
missed

avoiding

a perfectionist
examines

custody
of the eyes

his conscience

a twinkle

a spider web

        stripped down

bears the weight

        to bare essentials

of angels

        the word for
        fallen

what is truth?

                    compass points

embroidered
patches

                    sewn through
                    the fabric

of autumn
leaves

                    of the news

light
no more

        an absence

than the fall
of words

        less sought for
        than known

from the lips

        in the letting go

wolf hour

        drizzle-drench day

black swans
drift between

        cold
        cuts in keener

sleep
and non-sleep

        than a sword

where wind
starts

         Yemeni
         famine

the colour
of a rainbow

         a dandelion
         shivers

in the night

         to the last
         breath

sixth extinction

       the scent

our house
of cards

       of something
       long forgotten

sculpted of ice

       an instant
       before

the plip plop

a silence

of new absences

not of
dusk's unmaking

pock the earth

hushes
the frog

Ko Te Kore (the void, energy, nothingness, potential)
Te Kore-te-whiwhia (the void in which nothing is possessed)
Te Kore-te-rawea (the void in which nothing is felt)
Te Kore-i-ai (the void with nothing in union)
Te Kore-te-wiwia (the space without boundaries)
Na Te Kore Te Po (from the void the night)
Te Po-nui (the great night)
Te Po-roa (the long night)
Te Po-uriuri (the deep night)
Te Po-kerekere (the intense night)
Te Po-tiwhatiwha (the dark night)
Te Po-te-kitea (the night in which nothing is seen)
Te Po-tangotango (the intensely dark night)
Te Po-whawha (the night of feeling)

not a word

        breathing
        symbols

pilgrim, shrine
& the mist

        for
        the Nameless

between
trees

        into verse

snowed under

> *my fingers*
> *tap out*

I sound out
the subtleties

> *the staccato*
> *of being*

of silence

> *a languaged*
> *being*

migrant
godwits

          words
          yield gently

sounding out
the beauty

          to the
          ultimate importance

of the
quotidian

          of the
          protean present

deeper yet

        mizu no oto

the stilling
silence

        the poetry
        lost within

to be
plumbed

        expectations

autumn's gloom

        after the quake

knocked down
and out

        the bird bath
        again

the chatter

        mirrors the sky

a measuring box
I bought

my breathing

my excuse for
changing my mind

becomes a prayer

about
moon viewing

distraction

chrysanthemum
scent

hoc est
corpus meum

in Nara
many ancient

words to make
a sacred absence

Buddhas

apparent

summer grasses

        regenerating
        bush

where warriors
left

        a spectral light
        filters

their dreams

        through young
        green leaves

on a
withered branch

shutting my eyes

a crow has come
home to roost

I hear the word
alight

the autumn gloom

my writer's block

night drizzle

             should I

listen to
the ponderings

             raise my eyes
             to her

of moss
& I

             passing scent?

a future
perfect

> *more & more*

soughs through
falling leaves

> *a lack of*
> *meaning*

which will
have been

> *between*
> *the lines*

clouds
of blossoms

        angelus bell

that temple bell

        I lower my eyes
        into

from Ueno?
or Asukusa?

        the inconceivable

for the present

        whisper-wise

I hearken to
the sound

        you have become
        the music

of your absence

        beyond our ken

short poems

       still unknown

honed to
instruments

       I fit

of silence

       right in

breath-taking

        unvoiced praise

the world
within's

        the world
        without

ins & outs

        a smeared rag

Anzac Day

                sharpening

I return
from the war

                an end
                to end

with my self

                all war

winter ends

        lingering darkness

my wisps
of words

        magpies question

to clouds,
a bird

        the dawn chorus

crawling out
of winter

        Bloomin' Dublin

the gnarled limbs

        the wonder
        of language

of my other
life

        wanderin' home

this twist
of light

    conjugating verbs
    to be

my beginnings
at being

    sometimes
    i forget

a pine
at dawn

    that
    i'm awake

Gamma Tucanae's
far-off light

            the inner
            darkness

as it was
at my birth

            as far as
            my words

now in sight

            dare take me

a moth

          moonless night

brushstroking
darkness

          just the sound
          of water

by candle light

          interiorised

silent vigil

my self
it speaks

my verses edge
the far edges

and spells
at last

of language

this
spendsavour salt

the year starts

        to utter it

my first words
first-foot

        holding
        the silence

near and far

        a new haiku

on
first reading

      a haiku

my willing
suspension

      aspires to be

of disbelief

      in my words

one word

        an echo

after another

        of an echo

in tandem

        so what!
        so what!

paling

        haiku pupil

into oblivion

        here
        for comparison

a day-moon

        a black hole

for want
of a voice

        a pregnant silence

a poem's
rhythmic shudder

        more lusted after
        than the words

through mid-breath
pauses

        with which
        to voice it

he has
broken free

        late summer kigo

from the master's
apron strings

        a poet
        formally forsakes

dry cicada shell

        both the tried
        & tired

blind
with words

       a poet
       sounds out

whispered
in darkness

       the songs
       being silenced

singed
with light

       breath
       by breath

dawn chorus

       facebook
       newsfeed

the song
of my waking

       I practice
       compassion

unattached
to anything

       without
       commitment

climate change

              I rename

I cave-in

              all my poem
              folders

to my
survival instinct

              as Dead Sea
              Scrolls

astir in light

        dawn chorus

my reflection
passes

        ecstatic utterance
        stills

through it

        my bird-mind

setting sun

        déjà ku

a redback

        a poet
        cannibalizes

widows herself

        the tried
        and true

our palms

a pretence

myr red in

of abiding presence

martian dust

on ochred walls

grounded

        another verse

in
the moment

        force-fed

my
next step

        on words

Elgar concerto

> *I am*
> *well-practised*

did I fall then
for du Pré

> *in the silence*
> *of my craft*

or her cello self?

> *or sullen art*

dawn aphasia

               the persistence
               of

the pervasive
silence
thaws

               a
               not
               her

into
wordlessness

               memory

passers-by

       distant surf

speaking
of reality

       all that I want
       to do

my verse
unfinished

       is sleep

blossoms
battering

            nothing

against
the tyranny

            breezing through

of language

            the gaps

in the mist

        the dream
        of words

a swan's
shy and secret

        by the cold light
        of stars

complexity

        voices
        silence

morning mist

        the wind turbine

prayer charges
the air

        postdates
        a breath

with white noise

        of fresh air

morning mist

        a new name

litanies of cancers
miming

        written on
        a white stone

litanies of loss

        foreshore
        & seabed

longest night

                late-life
                poems

the unseen
remains

                time
                stretches out

to be seen

                in a metaphor

vanishing point

beside each other

a morepork's
name-calling

yet equidistant

thins out
the silence

*haiku
perspective*

one foot

             thin-skinned

after
the other

             I navigate
             beyond

pedestrian
verse

             my limits

between
twin towers

my pen
wordless

of babble

penetrates
the veneer

words breach
the limits

of meaning

just
a haiku poet

      God's silence

sucking up
the milky way

      catching a breath
      paused

through
a straw

      in
      its incompleteness

sea-born
psalm

        words shuffle

a cadence
hovers

        along
        parallel lines

the horizon

        one breath
        to another

in the beginning

        my daughter

was the word

        teasing out
        the narrative

yet to be
uttered

        of a
        möbius strip

pond surface

                my daughter

a cloud seen

                regards the world

for what
it is

                without
                language

words connect

        a peripheral
        tear

with the logic

        in the fabric

of the moist eye

        of space
        and time

amorous night

          I name fire
          fire

conjuring
neither fire

          from the dark
          memory

nor brimstone

          of eons
          and tribes

meiosis

a parent
verse

we feast
on five loaves

goes forth
and multiplies

and two fish

by division

bee-loud tree

ecstatic utterance

my daughter
and I

we escape
the ordinariness

voice
the same
silences

of merely waiting

summer pasture

                just poems

a dream
that remains

                formerly
                known as

of warring
words

                haiku

holy mountain

> *silence*
> *erupts in song*

I leave
my baser instincts

> *from*
> *my voicelessness*

at base camp

> *before the stars*

fleet-fingered

          found wanting

an autistic child

          the music
          of the spheres

indexes
the cosmos

          throws
          a wobbly

unfurl
within me

fetid
with life

fern-scolls
of prophecy

all beauty
festers

chanting
light

with
retracted claws

Otaki Beach

mythic chant

the cosmic
silence

stillness
roaming about

roaring
within words

lonely places

Anzac Cove

the warring
dead

the blood
of poppies

stilled
cannon fodder

to dull
the pain

of empire

a mosquito

    what is not yet

leaps the length

    pierces my heart

of our caresses

    with its absence

a moth

        moonless night

brushstroking
darkness

        just the sound
        of water

by candle light

        interiorized

viral verse

ars poetica

rising from
deep within

the leap frog

an interior
castle

*from pond
to sound*

ubi ubu?

"merdre!"

ubi vultures
colligentes

dada squeezes
a turd

ubi ibi est

from his words

beyond
being

        immune

useful members
of society

        to herd mentality

autumn leaves

        this secret room

night meniscus

       hidden depths

arcing synapses

       secreted from

spill it all

       my verse's pores

string quartet

        last movement

each instrument
in turn

        the silence
        storming

sounds
the ineffable

        everything

a blacksmith

        tender shoots

hammers out
the hard edges

        of long buried
        psalms

of kindness

        en-chant me

twin towers

       phallic wonders

lest mammon
understands

       Romulus & Remus
       babble brotherhood

the crescent moon

       in other tongues

yes

        a comma

and yet

        nuzzles into

a yes

        the stream

a fly
by

word play

Issa
wringing

*a noun
& a verb*

both
hands

*vie for
ascendancy*

misty rain

      an image

becoming

      siphoned
      from one soul

utterance

      to another

neither nor

       I rephrase

a stillborn's

       known
       platitudes

afterbirth

       with wizened
       words

sans eyes
sans teeth

        mewling
        and puking

the verses
I craft

        as a nursling
        born

for
dulled ears

        into
        mere oblivion

seventy-one

delivery suite

dare I end
that line

I embody
the poems

with
an ellipsis?

yet to be

same old
same old

        apparition

keeping it
consistent

        at a metro
        station

making in
new

        petals
        on black

vespers with

ancient chants

breath wisps of

conjuring faith

aspirations

in my own tongue

a pyre crafted

                    myth-making erupts

of old poems
en-kindling

                    from the rag
                    and bone shop

a storm shelter

                    of the hardened
                    heart

light
no more

        an absence

than the fall
of words

        less sought for
        than known

from the lips

        in the letting go

at its heart

        in deeper water

an everlasting ache

        my message
        in a bottle

freed from words

        bobs beside
        the plimsoll line

my child's
eyes

fleeting light

bursting
at the seams

our rosetta stone

with silence

of language

a sign

        uncrossed

intoned
by name

        the poet's voice

three
in one

        peters out

Ko Te Kore (the void, energy, nothingness, potential)
Te Kore-te-whiwhia (the void in which nothing is possessed)
Te Kore-te-rawea (the void in which nothing is felt)
Te Kore-i-ai (the void with nothing in union)
Te Kore-te-wiwia (the space without boundaries)
Na Te Kore Te Po (from the void the night)
Te Po-nui (the great night)
Te Po-roa (the long night)
Te Po-uriuri (the deep night)
Te Po-kerekere (the intense night)
Te Po-tiwhatiwha (the dark night)
Te Po-te-kitea (the night in which nothing is seen)
Te Po-tangotango (the intensely dark night)
Te Po-whawha (the night of feeling)
Te Po-namunamu-ki-taiao (the night of seeking the passage to the world)
Te Po-tahuri-atu (the night of restless turning)
Te Po-tahuri-mai-ki-taiao (the night of turning towards the revealed world)

ahh death!

        from a pretence

so much content
emptied

        of enduring
        presence

into
a single word

        we strain into
        the past tense

ahh life!

       less than all

an unapproachable
light

       a vision
       of perfection

nests
within us

       briefly glimpsed

out of nothing

such a big bang

the word
to be spoken

the energy
it takes

within us

to be seen

early days

                the genesis

my helpmate
& I

                of knowing
                & living

all gardened
out

                out of kilter

if
[nothing less than kind]

       I forfeit

    then
[strings of anything]

       the ordering
       of leaves

    else[s ….]
:end if

       to an hesitance
       in dying

a raindrop's

if autumn

conditional
branching

*then leaves
may fall*

down
the pane

*no longer
alone*

deathly still

      night vigil

worn out
with wailing

      a man re-enters

last night's wind

      his birth cry

nature calls

        far removed

I recycle
the by-products

        a blackbird
        ticks off

of being
me

        the end
        of days

words for
what is

       ear to
       the rail

trained along
parallel lines

       I listen for
       the sound

to their
vanishing points

       of whispering
       death

in
the garden

*a falling
leaf*

a poppy
closes

*ferries
another
species*

as the night
inhales me

*to the
was-land*

a levity
of light

a wind
blows in

alights
upon

from the vast
emptiness

the open
casket

I return to
my unknown self

decrepit
shadows

        the history

darkening
the urupā's

        of my
        native land

hidden
mounds

        only
        skin deep

heart to heart

                enfolded

the worm

                in blushing joy

and the rose

                our little death

rosary vigil

   quite unnoticed

rattling through
the mysteries

   in Breughel's
   Icarus

she lived for

   it was
   spring

the art of haiku boils down to this:

shadows

        a toothless old man

emerging
from the fog

        sucking marrow

while light
dies

        from the skeleton
        of words

deathbed watch

                here
                and now

a candle flame
enters

                the silence
                in seeing

the night wind

                awaits
                utterance

unadorned

       mountain-viewing

unaccommodated

       ancestral bone-dust

me

       being itself

the pearl
within

                with bright eyes

the all
for which

                an unadorned
                bride

I go
without

                above
                rubies

it's dead
certain

       lung cancer

a substantial
change

       I watch a friend
       go up

in the wind

       in smoke

daily stream

        Lenten fast

our communion

        I forgo

wholly spiritual

        a normal life

black hole
viewing

Lenten frugality

shall I
serialise

*I enquire
about dying*

my sense
of self?

*on an
instalment plan*

summer grasses

                    in the garden

the earth
gorges on

                    vegetables
                    break out

blood
and bone

                    of their
                    mass graves

last quarter

        the grief
        shed

an apple
we shared

        lies drowned

also betokens
loss

        within
        shallow graves

feathered wind

       ritual death

moonrise hatches

       who will I be

a myth

       when I awaken?

soughing wind

                the damsel
                with a dulcimer

a night caller
briefly glimpsed

                single artificer

seems at one
with it

                of beatific vision

gravity
and grace

> *savaged*
> *to extinction*

a pilot whale
yearns towards

> *the moist eye*
> *of being*

a tender
death

> *at one*
> *with the all*

paddling

        a fetal dream

my own canoe

        slouching
        to Bethlehem

all the
either-ors

        my end
        in sight

death rattle

       a mythic child

the sound
concreted

       rides an
       empty see-saw

down under

       into the moon

cosmic
loneliness

while we sleep

a dandelion
enfolded

the ever-present
blue

under
the milky way

of a
smartphone

through
the eyes

in the end

of a mayfly

a period
executes

the mosaic
of life

its death
sentence.

this hour

chill night

in which
the wolf

an absence of terror

is but a word

warms to me

holy souls

       deep-down dark

between
one mystery

       swimming within
       the ever-hidden

and the next

       shadows

receding light

        at dead low
        water

my interior
landscape's

        where meaning
        lies

inverse presence

        and distance
        ends

the ploughman's

                rhythm sprung

slow
iambic feet

                from
                a metronome

plod on home

                winding down

caught
off-guard

                a violin strains

the divine light

                to hold
                my breath

of the moon

                a little longer

Advent candle

> *the amount*
> *of earth*

the stillness
of death

> *to fill up*
> *a grave slot*

but a whisper
away

> *six feet deep*

self-sown
tomato

        man-scarred
        landscape

love pitches
its tent

        cementing
        the illusion

in no
enduring city

        of glass
        seen through

viral endgame

        a rocking cradle

the reign
of the alpha

        vexed again
        to nightmare

and of
the omega

        from stony sleep

the clarity

       all around

in spring rain

       your presence
       fills up

of being
seen

       my blind spot

last post

      and the you
      we knew

a chill wind
sounds

      at one
      once more

the bugle

      with your
      namelessness

lisp-synching

among
the epitaphs

a soft sussuration
of words

ancestral spirits

through
leaf scrolls

blood
the earth

headstone

                end of time.

I used to
know you

                the mystery
                of God

by heart

                is
                finished

dusk light

        my hands
        remember

the sacred
gathers

        the touch
        of each hand

all around

        they once held

the world
such as it is

        sweet darkness!

defiantly present

        I love
        the chiaroscuro

in assemblages
of after-images

        your manifestation
        obscures

which
comes first

       glaucoma

herd immunity

       my tunneling
       vision

or my death?

       looks to
       the end

rain again

                sad stories

the trickle
of the divine

                pitter-pattering
                the earth

down
my face

                with the death
                of kings

washed-out
clouds

        in a
        dreamscape

on the horizon

        I witness
        the leavetaking

washed-out
lands

        of Sylvia Plath's
        ghost

with dewfall

        in its wings

the hidden life
eludes

        already
        the butterfly's

the early bird

        afterlife

Advent
communion

after the storm

who can tally
the losses

the Book of Job
breaks open

being poured
forth

to the
fog's swirl

figures
in light

a wind farm

an anchor
of images

becomes the last
remaining

shakes us
free

sign
of God

an epitaph

        all questions

unwritten
as yet

        about human
        & divine

scrolls
unread

        laid
        to rest

Ko Te Kore (the void, energy, nothingness, potential)
Te Kore-te-whiwhia (the void in which nothing is possessed)
Te Kore-te-rawea (the void in which nothing is felt)
Te Kore-i-ai (the void with nothing in union)
Te Kore-te-wiwia (the space without boundaries)
Na Te Kore Te Po (from the void the night)
Te Po-nui (the great night)
Te Po-roa (the long night)
Te Po-uriuri (the deep night)
Te Po-kerekere (the intense night)
Te Po-tiwhatiwha (the dark night)
Te Po-te-kitea (the night in which nothing is seen)
Te Po-tangotango (the intensely dark night)
Te Po-whawha (the night of feeling)
Te Po-namunamu-ki-taiao (the night of seeking the passage to the world)
Te Po-tahuri-atu (the night of restless turning)
Te Po-tahuri-mai-ki-taiao (the night of turning towards the revealed world)

Ki te Whai-ao (to the glimmer of dawn)
Ki te Ao-marama (to the bright light of day)
Tihei mauri-ora (there is life)

bereft
for now

> *my soul*
> *(my deer)*

still shall I
ever know

> *deep calls*
> *to deep*

ever
belonging

> *in the*
> *cascade's roar*

sunflowers

        December moon

are my arms
opening

        the body
        and blood

more to light?

        living in me

a newborn
lamb

I heard

bleats for
the loneliness

silence tonight

it once knew

it was
wondrous

here

        the ins
        & outs

in the one

        of white
        light

ever-present
now

        prisming
        what passed

a rock pool

        the reflection

in and
for itself

        of a love
        divine

here
& now

        in waiting

words
are fake

I hear

truth lies
within

the authentic

shape-shifting
clouds

in visions

light lisps

        out of
        the depths

off the lips

        wordless groans
        clamouring

of this pair

        to give birth

amateur philologist
that I am

       a moot point

beloved

       the loving silence

of the Word

       in my daughter's
       eyes

if lent

        in my palm

& not
owned

        you are indeed

a soul's
metanoia

        a great leap

my image

> *not seeing*
> *eye to eye*

caged in
the panther's heart

> *another part*
> *of us*

ceases
to be

> *dies*
> *today*

the third rite

      hushed tones

last year's
fig leaves

      Virgil
      guides Dante

fall away

      canto
      by canto

pure
soundlessness

musica
universalis

I listen beyond
the sounds

after-images
of the sublime

of my
listlessness

dance along
my pulse

as it was
in the beginning

                albatross
                of light

is now

                Christ

and ever
shall be

                I am
                the ocean

here I am
Lord

                    blossoms too

my hunger
ready to gnaw

                    will exist
                    as echoes

into
your pronoun

                    of my cry

a pregnant
passage

    cede your mind

seeded
with symbolism

    as awakened
    words

sprung from
unknowing

    read me
    to you

awakened

         ministrations
         of misery

by a
cabbage white

         a rotting orange
         dangles

laying eggs

         from the tree
         of life

deepest night

        Easter Week

the coalsack
nebula

        an absence
        hidden by

clouds
a vision

        the Southern
        Cross

praying hands

                a tree trunk

between them
I hide

                hollowed
                of meaning

in nothingness

                yields to things
                ageless

same old valley

        it's all
        about me

a transfiguring
moon

        thy kingdom
        that is not

silences me

        of this world

for Christ's sake

                a spark

not only
human nature

                divined from

but also

                the slime

make a name
for yourself

*with tongue-tripping
skips*

imprint
your presence
into

*from lips
to petrichor*

our hearts
of stone

*rain's
pitter-patter*

a quickening

Easter Dawn

at the
darkest before . . .

*let he
who has no life*

empty husk

*rise
to the challenge*

roadside shrines

        a clay figure

weathered
to indistinction

        I remember
        being shaped

in unceasing
prayer

        to take
        a breath

a godwit
freshly returned

the dark night

pores through

painting
a self-portrait

its hieroglyphic
record

of the unseen god

a night wind

        on the wall

rages against
the walls

        unaccommodated
        man

of domestic
bliss

        hung
        on a cross

freshwater
fountain

fifty years on

the thirsting
god

*the gap
you speak of*

rising
in us

*yes
I find it so*

morning mass

        pebble-bottomed
        streams

the breath
of God

        lisp lightly
        for pyres

rings
a bellbird

        of barely-seen
        stars

all matter

fleshing out
the heard

all energy
all space

with head-bowing
reverence

briefly
dwelt in

the angelus bell

the long wait
done

        newborn love

the unknowable

        stillness moves
        the cosmos

enters time

        beyond
        emptiness

longest night

        crucifix

no moon
to dull down

        a word
        to incarnate

the vast sky

        an apparent
        absence

a child places

        wild winds

a finger
to her lips

        writing
        the wrongs

while God
whispers

        in a wordless
        language

wolf hour

        brow-beaten
        by night

the mind
of Christ
blooms

        my self-image

in my garden

        sweats blood

by autumn
dusk

*the seen
unknown*

this tree
imagined
becomes

*risen
into knowing*

the wholly
real

*at the breaking
of bread*

"se-woo, ha-nah e-too-hee pagh-ri"

primal light

                a spotless host

the empyrean

                consumed with
                simple words

born out of
the mundane

                of self-immolation

not yet blind

> *still point*

space defined
by the stretch

> *a consecrated host*

of my mind's
cane

> *lightens*
> *my palm*

without
a doubt

           embodying
           God

a tree
without

           neither the ends
           of thought

and
within

           nor the
           in-betweens

so much depends
upon

       panis angelicus

a little red hen

       fulfilling
       all metaphors

earning
her crust

       we become
       what we receive

bread
and wine

       the words

an illusion
of being

       severally
       and impossibly

made
apparent

       become flesh

puddled
night

our lenten
reflection

I peer
down
deeper

broken down
into only

into stars

two
dimensions

compline

we enter

shadows seize
my breath

our perfect
expression

in
soundlessness

without
words

clouding
over

        a salamander

a moment's
infused

        has laid
        its eggs

contemplation

        in my
        mind's eye

deepening
darkness

de profundis

the sanctuary
candle's

a quiet
alchemy

sacrificial
light

quickens
my soul

in the wish

        a drop
        of water

to become
present to you

        creases

I become so

        into
        the wine

"I thirst"

darkest
before dawn

this chalice
drained

easter in me

to the last
drop

with open wounds

the ascension

       at Akitio

of the hypostatic
union

       a poet
       transcribing eternity

to the all
in all

       from the ocean

the silence

                sometimes
                joy

a holy hush
resonating

                will spill
                from my eyes

through
the fury

                and wet
                my beard

Do you remember yet the moment that I will be asking whether you remember this moment when I am asking you if you remember while I am placing my palm against a silhouetted hand on a cave wall long after we will be sharing this memory? It had always been in the process of becoming the time when the double helical grip of my DNA has shaped the holy ground into which I will, in retrospect, have been descending.

autumn . . .

        boundless forms

my shadow into

        sculpted
        from within
        light's

a cloud's

        self-effacement

ACKNOWLEDGMENTS

Many thanks to the editors of *Otata, Bones, Sonic Boom, Under the Bashō, Heliosparrow Poetry Journal, & Lothlorien Poetry Journal.* Many of these poems (or earlier versions of them) were first curated in these journals.

Authorship was ascribed to me under my *nom de plume* (*Hansha Teki*) which I had been using for the time being.

"It is a joy and a source of constant wonder and afterthought to witness how Stephen Bailey has made the parallel (haiku) work for his own writing with excellence. If anything this is a deeply spiritual book grounded in the writer's journey towards the silence in which God speaks to the soul and his sensing of The Other in all things and all aspects of his life. *For the Time Being* is a book to be read again and again."

—Johannes S. H. Bjerg – writer, artist, editor

"Possibly the most significant development in haiku-influenced poetry in our generation, these are both intensely personal and metaphysical poems – The very heart of becoming – in which the poem exceeds its own form, attaining something much larger."

—Eric Selland – poet, translator

"In Stephen Bailey's parallel poems we enter a liminal space, where time unfolds the mysteries of our origins in the echoes of now. For Bailey, we are forever becoming within the shift and pull of nature and human nature. These are poems of sunlight and shadow, and all the glimmerings in between."

—Patricia Nelson – poet, artist

"Over the years, Stephen Bailey has carved a niche for himself, finding a distinctive voice while working in the form of the parallel haiku. With *For The Time Being,* Bailey has uttered a major artistic statement in the genre of the short poem. This impressive collection is the culmination of one man's journey and a lifetime of developing his craft.

For The Time Being reaches into the primordial memories of the collective unconscious to explore the act of being. With an autumnal, contemplative tone, it strips away masks and touches a sense of the timeless and eternal. Serenely beautiful and deeply mysterious, Bailey has crafted a gnostic reverie in the spaces between lines. In the interstices between images, these brief contrapuntal poems create a sense of infinite space out of just a few words. Masterfully minimalist, this collection of verse is spiritual, moving, and memorable."

—Clayton Beach – poet, editor